Karen's LOL Jokes Collection

The 2 Books Compilation Set For Kids

Karen J. Bun

This book consists of:

1. Karen's OMG Joke Books For Kids - Funny, Silly, Dumb Jokes that Will Make Children Roll on the Floor Laughing
2. Karen's Dad Jokes - The Bad, Funny, Clean And LOL Jokes For The Cool Dad

Karen's OMG Joke Book for Kids

Funny, Silly, Dumb Jokes that Will Make Children Roll on the Floor Laughing

Karen J. Bun

Table of Contents

Bluesource And Friends

This book is brought to you by Bluesource And Friends, a happy book publishing company.

Our motto is **"Happiness Within Pages."**

We promise to deliver amazing value to readers with our books.

We also appreciate honest book reviews from our readers.

Connect with us on our Facebook page www.facebook.com/bluesourceandfriends and stay tuned to our latest book promotions and free giveaways.

Don't forget to claim your FREE book

https://tinyurl.com/karenbrainteasers

Also check out our best seller book

https://tinyurl.com/lateralthinkingpuzzles

Introduction

Congratulations on downloading the book *Karen's OMG Joke Book for Kids: Funny, Silly, Dumb Jokes that Will Make Children Roll on the Floor Laughing.* I thank you for downloading it. The following chapters will make your child howl with laughter. The first chapter is filled with riddles that will make their sides hurt. This book has everything from the classic knock-knock jokes to bad puns that will make even you shake your head! There are also a few surprises along the way! Your child will read some 'quirky questions' as well as 'books never written.' This book was designed for kids between the ages of seven and twelve. They will experience short, sweet, and simple jokes as well as longer jokes that grab their attention and deliver a forceful one-liner!

There are plenty of books like this on the market, so thanks again for choosing this one! Every effort was made to ensure your child will enjoy what they are about to read. Please enjoy!

Chapter 1 Kids' Riddles

Q: My outside can be thrown and my inside can be cooked. My outside can be eaten and my inside can be thrown. What am I?

A: A corn's cob. The stalk is thrown and the corn is cooked. The inside can be thrown once the corn has been eaten.

Q: I have three hands but I cannot use them to clap. What am I?
A: I'm a clock.

Q: You can only use me once you have broken me. What am I?
A: I'm an egg.

Q: I can't see even though I still have an eye. What do you think I am?
A: A needle

Q: The most water can only be held by what letter?
A: The 'C'

Q: There was a blue, one-story house. The couch was blue. The rugs were blue. Even the cat was blue. What color do you think the stairs were?

A: The house didn't have any stairs. It was only one-story.

Q: All through winter, I have lived. Once I die during summer, roots start to grow from the top. What am I?
A: An ice cycle

Q: Even the world's strongest person can't hold this for more than sixty seconds although it is as light as a feather. What is it?
A: They can't hold their breath.

Q: A cowboy rode into town on Wednesday. He stayed for three days and left the same town on Wednesday. How can this be possible?
A: The cowboy's horse's name is Wednesday.

Q: How is it possible for a person to go without sleep for 8 days straight?
A: They only sleep at night.

Q: Moneyless people have this and it is needed by wealthy people. You will eventually die once you've eaten it. What is it?
A: It's nothing.

Q: Which has more weight, a pound of cement or a pound of paper?
A: Both of them weigh a pound, so they are equal.

Q: What is used more by other people but is always yours?

A: Your name

Q: I can't open doors even though I'm full of keys. What am I?

A: I'm a piano.

Q: I have four fingers and one thumb, but I am not a living thing.
What am I?

A: A glove

Q: How many months in the year have twenty-eight days in them?

A: All of the months have twenty-eight days!

Q: Which invention helps you to see through walls?

A: A window

Q: What occurs one time in a minute, two times in a moment, and
never in 100 years?

A: 'M'

Q: As it dries, it gets wetter?

A: A towel gets wetter as it dries.

Q: Everyone has one of these, and it is impossible to lose. What is it?

A: A shadow

Q: How much distance can be run by a fox into the woods?
A: Only halfway. Otherwise, it would be running out of the woods.

Q: Take away a single letter, I become even. At first, I'm very odd.
What am I?
A: Seven

Q: This will never fall back down but will always go up.
A: Your age

Q: What word has a T and starts and ends with a T?
A: It's a teapot.

Q: I get shorter as I get old, although when I was young, I am tall.
What am I?
A: A candle

Q: What word is spelled wrong in every single dictionary?
A: Wrong

Q: I start with the letter 'E', and I only have one letter in me. What
am I?
A: I'm an envelope.

Q: How does a leopard change its spots?
A: It gets up and moves to a different one.

Q: What is really hard to get out of but super easy to get into?
A: Trouble

Q: If a mom, a dad, and their son were not underneath an umbrella, how did they not get wet?
A: It wasn't raining.

Q: Troy's parents had three sons. They were named Snap, Crackle, and what?
A: Troy

Q: You bought me for dinner, but you have never eaten me. What am I?
A: A fork and knife

Q: After a train crashed, every single person died. Who survived?
A: All of the couples

Q: I still can't see even though I have four eyes.
A: Mississippi

Q: Even though I'm staying in the same spot, I can still travel all around the world. What do you think am I?
A: A stamp

Q: The English alphabet contains how many letters?
A: There are eighteen. 3 in 'the', 7 in 'English', and 8 in 'alphabet'.

Q: I can still hold liquid even though I have holes. What am I?
A: A sponge

Q: What can you never answer yes to?
A: Are you asleep?

Q: When everything seems to be going wrong, what can you always count on?
A: Your fingers can always be counted.

Q: What's always ahead of you but you can never see?
A: The future

Q: Where can you find, cities, towns, countries, and shops but no people?
A: A map

Q: Bob walked for half an hour in the rain and didn't get a hair on his head wet. He didn't have an umbrella or a hat. How did he do it?
A: He is bald.

Q: I cannot hear even though I have ears. What am I?
A: Corn

Q: There are no doors or windows in this kind of room. What room is this?
A: A mushroom

Q: What do you take in when it isn't being used, but throw out when you need to use it?
A: An anchor

Q: I have difficulty standing up by myself even though I have thousands of legs. I don't have a head even if my neck is long. What am I?
A: I'm a broom.

Q: I can't walk although I have legs.
A: A table

Q: What never moves but always goes up?
A: Stairs

Q: Which side does an egg fall when it was laid by a rooster at the top of a barn?

A: A rooster can't lay eggs. Hens do.

Q: When is a door not a door?

A: When it's ajar

Q: You can't hold me. You can only catch me. What am I?

A: A cold

Q: What can be deadly and quick while it gathers by the beach?

A: Sand

Q: Be careful! You are at a railroad crossing. Be sure that there are no cars. Can you spell this without any 'r's'?

A: T-H-I-S

Q: I have no door, but I hold keys. I have no place to stay even though I have some space. You aren't allowed to leave even if you can enter me. What am I?

A: I'm a keyboard.

Q: I can run and drop but can't walk. What am I?

A: A drop of water

Q: If there are five apples and you take two, how many do you have?
A: You have two.

Q: I have wings, and I can fly. I am not a bird, so what am I?
A: An airplane

Q: What is always late and never present?
A: Later

Q: I can be big, white, dirty, or wicked. What am I?
A: A lie

Q: What do cats, dogs, fish, and turtles all have in common?
A: The letter 'S'

Q: Almost everybody needs me, asks for me, gives me but hardly anyone takes me. What am I?
A: Advice

Q: What am I that can point in every direction, but I can't get anywhere by myself?
A: Your finger

Q: I am not your clothes, but I cover your body. What am I that get thinner the more that I am used?

A: A bar of soap

Q: What am I that never break even if I fall?

A: Nightfall

Q: I'm known as the first of all of my kind. I am never found in trucks and never on buses. I'm not used in Ohio, but I am used in Arkansas.

A: The letter 'A'

Q: I have two backbones and thousands upon thousands of ribs.

A: A railroad

Q: I will always point you in the right direction. You must follow my lead or you will get astray. What am I that will never say more than two words at a time?

A: The signage of 'one way'

Q: I can run constantly without getting tired. I frustrate people without having to move. What am I?

A: A runny nose

Q: What am I that the more of me you leave behind, the more of me
you take.

A: I'm footsteps.

Q: I'm heavy forward, but backward I am not. What am I?

A: I'm a ton.

Q: What am I that get bigger the more you've taken from me?

A: I'm a hole.

Q: What am I that if I'm with you, you will want to tell me. But once
you tell me, I am no longer with you.

A: I'm a secret.

Q: Everyone has a view of me but doesn't pay attention. Without
one, though, everyone would look crazy. What am I?

A: I'm a nose.

Q: It will be harder for you to grab me the more you move with me.

A: Your breath

Q: Do what he says, and you will be okay. Don't and you will lose the
game. Who is he?

A: Simon

Q: Bugs don't like this vegetable. It may be the only one they don't move toward. What is it?
A: It's a squash.

Q: You can see me in the water sometimes, but I am always dry.
A: A reflection

Q: I only repeat the last word you say. The more I repeat, the softer I get. I can't be seen but I can be heard. What am I?
A: An echo

Q: Take me for a spin, and I will make you cool. If you use me in the winter, you are a fool. What am I?
A: A fan

Q: You can't really see me, but you can touch me. You can't throw me away but you can throw me out.
A: Your back

Q: What am I that will halt on green and continue on red when you are dealing with me?
A: I'm a watermelon.

Q: Shadows follow me wherever I go. I have no eyes but I can produce tears. I have no wings but I can glide above you. What am I?

A: I'm a cloud.

Q: He says I love you when I told him. He smiles back at me when I smile at him and looks back at me when I look at him. Who is he?
A: His reflection

Q: I go around all cities, towns, and villages but I never go inside anywhere.
A: A road

Q: What do you think I am that can die when I have no life?
A: A battery

Q: When you wave my flag, I took and give away the one you receive?
A: I'm a mailbox.

Q: I'm a five-letter word and very big and hard. I am alone when two letters are removed from me.
A: Stone

Q: I know a word that has six letters. Take away just one letter, twelve is what remains. What word am I?
A: Dozens

Q: Wash me and then I'm not clean. Don't wash me and I am.

A: Water

Q: I live without needing to breathe but I'm always cold. I am never dehydrated but I am hardly ever drinking. What am I?
A: I'm a fish.

Q: At the same time, I go down and up. I am present-tense and past-tense, too. What am I?
A: See-saw

Q: I always run, but there is no way I can walk. I sometimes make small noises but I am not talking. I also have a bed, but I never use it. I never eat but I have a mouth. What am I?
A: A river

Q: When I am changing my jacket, loud noises will be made. I begin to weigh less the more I become larger. What am I?
A: Popcorn

Q: What am I that becomes dirty when I'm white.
A: A blackboard

Q: I shave 30 times a day, but I still have hair.
A: A barber

Q: I do not have a head, but I have a long straight neck. What am I?

A: A bottle

Q: I stay where I am when I go off. What am I?

A: An alarm clock

Q: I do not ask questions but I need an answer.

A: A telephone

Q: What am I that go up and down all of the time, but I never move?

A: The temperature

Q: What do you think I am when I am weightless and as large as an elephant? What am I?

A: I'm an elephant's shadow.

Q: It is not wanted by the person who carved it. It's not needed yet by the person who bought it. It was never seen by the person who used it. What is this thing?

A: A coffin

Q: What do you call a thing that has a head and a foot but has 4 legs?

A: A bed

Q: You can never eat me for lunch or dinner. What am I?

A: Breakfast

Q: What do you call me when you can hold me without touching me?

A: A conversation

Q: I don't need to eat but I have teeth. What do you call me?

A: A comb

Q: What do you call something that can be made but cannot be seen?

A: Noise

Q: Orange is my color and I sound like a parrot. What am I?

A: Carrot

Q: I have flies and four wheels. What do you call me?

A: A garbage pick-up truck

Q: Which part of the turkey has the most feathers?

A: The outside

Chapter 2: Kids' Knock-Knock Jokes

Knock, knock

Who's there?

Figs.

Figs who?

Figs the doorbell, it's not working right!

Knock, knock

Who's there?

Beef.

Beef who?

Beefore it gets too cold, let me in!

Knock, knock

Who's there?

Lettuce.

Lettuce who?

Lettuce inside!

Knock, knock

Who's there?

Olive.

Olive who?

Olive next door?

Knock, knock
Who's there?
Ice cream.
Ice cream who?
Ice cream for ice cream!

Knock, knock
Who's there?
Turnip.
Turnip who?
Turnip the volume, I can't hear anything!

Knock, knock
Who's there?
Orange.
Orange who?
Orange you working on your project?

Knock, knock

Who's there?
Mustache
Mustache who?

I mustache you something but I'll shave it for later if you won't open
the door for me!

Who's there?
Annie.
Annie who?
You don't believe Annie thing I say!

Knock, knock
Who's there?
Voodoo.
Voodoo who?
Voodoo you want to go with on your prom?

Knock, knock
Who's there?
Candice.
Candice who?
Candice be the right thing to say?

Knock, knock
Who's there?
Donut.
Donut who?
Donut ask anyone around here.

Knock, knock

Who's there?

Ada.

Ada who?

Ada spaghetti on my meal.

Knock, knock

Who's there?

Anita.

Anita who?

Anita buy shoes, please?

Knock, knock

Who's there?

Annie.

Annie who?

Annie body going to let me in?

Knock, knock

Who's there?

Ben.

Ben who?

Ben singing that song three times. Cut it out already!

Knock, knock

Who's there?

Frank.

Frank who?

I want to Frank you for making me smile.

Knock, knock

Who's there?

Doris.

Doris who?

Doris open, come in.

Knock, knock

Who's there?

Howard.

Howard who?

Howard you guess what that is?

Knock, knock

Who's there?

Isabell.

Isabell who?

Isabell ringing? Somebody might be outside.

Knock, knock

Who's there?

Justin.

Justin who?

Justin town. I have to check on some things.

Knock, knock

Who's there?

Ken

Ken who?

Ken I have more soup, please?

Knock, knock

Who's there?

Lena.

Lena who?

Lena bit closer and you'll know who.

Knock, knock

Who's there?

Nana.

Nana who?

Nana my things are missing.

Knock, knock

Who's there?

Nobel,

Nobel who?

Nobel. That's why I have been knocking for quite some time now.

Knock, knock

Who's there?

Windy.

Windy who?

Windy dog ran, it bumped on my knee.

Knock, knock

Who's there?

Will.

Will who?

Will I meet the man of my dreams someday?

Knock, knock

Who's there?

Cow go.

Cow go who?

No, cow go moo! A cow never said who.

Knock, knock

Who's there?

Goat.

Goat who?

Goat to the pharmacy and buy me some medicine, please.

Knock, knock

Who's there?

Some bunny.

Some bunny who?

Some bunny has finally won the jackpot prize!

Knock, knock

Who's there?

Amarillo.

Amarillo who?

Amarillo kind friend.

Knock, knock

Who's there?

Amish.

Amish who?

Amish our old days.

Knock, knock

Who's there?

Avenue.

Avenue who?

Avenue done makeup before?

Knock, knock

Who's there?

Cash.

Cash who?

I prefer eating peanuts than cash who.

Knock, knock

Who's there?

Dishes.

Dishes who?

Dishes a great place you've got.

Knock, knock

Who's there?

Doctor.

Doctor who?

That is such a great show!

Knock, knock

Who's there?

I'm too short to reach the doorbell.

I'm too short to reach the doorbell who?

No, really. I'm too short.

Knock, knock

Who's there?

Dozen.

Dozen who?

Dozen one know who holds the keys?

Knock, knock

Who's there?

Leaf.

Leaf who?

Leaf him alone. He's wounded.

Knock, knock

Who's there?

Howl.

Howl who?

Howl you remember me when I'm gone?

Knock, knock

Who's there?

Needle.

Needle who?

Do you needle bit help on your homework?

Knock, knock

Who's there?

Police.

Police who?

Police, may I have some cash?

Knock, knock

Who's there?

Radio.

Radio who?

I'm coming up, either you're radio or not.

Knock, knock

Who's there?

Water.

Water who?

Water you doing out there?

Knock, knock

Who's there?

Tank.

Tank who?

Tank you for welcoming me here.

Knock, knock

Who's there?

Witches.

Witches who?

Witches the simplest method to use?

Knock, knock

Who's there?

Wooden shoe.

Wooden shoe who?

Wooden shoe be happier if she's here?

Knock, knock

Who's there?

Harry.

Harry who?

Harry now or else I'll leave you behind.

Knock, knock

Who's there?

Canoe.

Canoe who?

Canoe please help me carry these things?

Knock, knock

Who's there?

I am.

I am who?

How do you not know who you are!

Knock, knock

Who's there?

Yah.

Yah who?

Google is what I prefer.

Knock, knock

Who's there?

Alpaca.

Alpaca who?

Alpaca a first aid kit for our trip tomorrow just to be sure.

Knock, knock

Who's there?

See, you forgot me already!

Knock, knock

Who's there?

Owl says.

Owl says who?

Yes, they do.

Knock, knock

Who's there?

Kanga

Kanga who?

It's not kanga who, it's a kangaroo.

Knock, knock

Who's there?

Beats

Beats who?

Beats me.

Knock, knock

Who's there?

Deja.

Deja who?

Knock, knock

Knock, knock

Who's there?

A broken pencil.

A broken pencil who?

It's pointless, so don't worry about it.

Knock, knock

Who's there?

Europe.

Europe who?

No, I'm not a poo! You're the poo!

Knock, knock

Who's there?

Theodore.

Theodore who?

Theodore was open that's why the thief entered easily.

Knock, knock

Who's there?

Etchy.

Etchy who?

Bless you!

Knock, knock

Who's there?

Spell.

Spell who?

W-H-O.

Knock, knock

Who's there?

Mikey.

Mikey who?

I left Mikey on the car.

Knock, knock

Who's there?

Herd.

Herd who?

I herd you call my name. Why?

Knock, knock

Who's there?

Venice.

Venice who?

Venice she going to school?

Knock, knock

Who's there?

Iran.

Iran who?

Iran straight from the grocery store.

Knock, knock

Who's there?

Adore.

Adore who?

Adore is open last night.

Knock, knock

Who's there?

Orange.

Orange who?

Orange you going to say you love me before you leave?

Chapter 3: Kids' Silly, Dumb Jokes

Q: A sleeping dinosaur is called what?

A: A dino-snore!

Q: What is fast but loud and crunchy at the same time?

A: A rocket-chip!

Q: Why did the teddy bear pass on dessert?

A: He was stuffed!

Q: What has thousands of ears, but it cannot hear?

A: A cornfield!

Q: What did the left eye say to the right eye?

A: There's something between us and it smells!

Q: What do you get when you come across a vampire and a snowman?

A: Frost-bite!

Q: What was said to the fork by the plate?

A: Dinner is on me!

Q: What is the reason behind the small boy eating his homework?

A: He heard from his teacher that it was a piece of cake!

Q: When you are looking for something, why is it always in the last place you look?

A: Because when you find it, you stop looking for it!

Q: Two pickles fell out of a jar and onto the counter. What did one say to the other?

A: Dill with it.

Q: After eating their supper, how did the Dalmatians react?

A: That hit the spot!

Q: Why did the group of kids cross the park?

A: They needed to get to the other slide!

Q: How does a vampire start writing a letter?

A: Tomb it may concern!

Q: What do you call a droid that takes a different route?

A: R2 detour

Q: How do you stop the astronaut baby from crying?

A: You rocket back and forth!

Q: What was the witches' favorite subject in middle school?

A: Spelling!

Q: How do you make a lemon drop?

A: You let the lemon fall!

Q: What do you call a duck that gets 100% on all of its school projects?

A: A wise quacker!

Q: What kind of water cannot freeze?

A: Hot water!

Q: What sort of tree fits in your hand?

A: A palm tree!

Q: Why did the cracker go to the hospital?

A: Because he felt really crummy!

Q: Why did the baby strawberry start crying?

A: Because its mom and dad were in a jam!

Q: What was the question being asked to the mommy corn by the baby corn?

A: Where is popcorn?

Q: What is worse than raining cats and dogs?

A: Hailing taxis!

Q: Where would you find a penguin?

A: Wherever you lost him!

Q: Which animal is always at a baseball game?

A: A bat!

Q: What always falls in winter but never gets hurt?

A: Snow!

Q: What do you call a ghost's true love?

A: His ghoulfriend!

Q: What building in Los Angeles has the most stories?

A: The public library!

Q: How do you know the ocean is friendly or not?

A: See if it waves!

Q: What is a tornado's favorite game to play at parties?

A: Twister!

Q: How does the moon cut his hair?

A: Eclipse it!

Q: How do you get a squirrel to like you?
A: You gotta act like a nutcase!

Q: What do you call two birds in love?
A: Tweethearts!

Q: How does a scientist freshen his breath?
A: He experi-mints!

Q: How are false teeth like stars?
A: They come out at night!

Q: How can you tell a vampire is getting sick?
A: He starts coffin!

Q: Finding that in your apple, there's a complete worm is less bad than what?
A: Finding a worm cut in half! That means you already ate half!

Q: What is a computer's favorite snack?
A: Computer chips!

Q: What did the cow hear from the apple?

A: Nothing. Apples cannot speak!

Q: When does a cucumber become a pickle?
A: Whenever it goes through a jarring experience!

Q: What do you think of that new diner on the mood?
A: The food was okay, but the atmosphere was awful!

Q: What is the reason why a balloon cannot be given to Elsa?
A: The reason is that it will be let go by her!

Q: How do you make the octopus laugh?
A: With ten-tickles!

Q: What did the finger hear from the nose?
A: Don't pick on me anymore!

Q: Why did the little girl bring a ladder to school?
A: Because she wanted to go to high school!

Q: What is a vampire's favorite fruit?
A: A blood orange!

Q: What do elves learn in English class?
A: The elf-abet!

Q: Why can't the karaoke be sung by the pony?

A: Because his voice was a little hoarse!

Q: Why are school dances being avoided by the skeleton?

A: Because he had no body to dance with!

Q: What do you call a pair of bananas?

A: Slippers

Q: Why is the doctor visited by the banana?

A: Because the banana doesn't peel well.

Q: A fake noodle is called what?

A: An impasta!

Q: How do you fix a cracked pumpkin?

A: You use a pumpkin patch!

Q: What sort of award did the dentist receive?

A: A little plaque!

Q: A sticky hair is a characteristic of bees because?

A: A honeycomb is what they use!

Q: An example of bad liars is the ghost. What is the reason for this?

A: Because they are transparent!

Q: How was the small flower greeted by the big flower?

A: Hey, bud!

Q: What did the astronaut say when he crashed into the planet?

A: I Apollo-gize!

Q: Why did the orange lose the race?

A: He ran out of juice!

Q: Which dinosaur has the best vocabulary?

A: The thesaurus!

Q: What did one strand of DNA say to her boyfriend strand of DNA?

A: Do these genes make my butt look big?

Q: Why didn't the dogs want to dance at the ball?

A: They have two left feet!

Q: What was being said to the toilet friend from a healthy toilet?

A: You seem a bit flushed!

Q: What is the reason the woman put her money in the freezer?

A: She wanted some cold hard cash!

Q: Why couldn't the astronaut book a room on the moon?

A: Because the moon was full!

Q: What do you call a snowman that is getting old?

A: Water!

Q: Why did the superhero flush his toilet?

A: Because it was his doody!

Q: Where do cows go for entertainment?

A: The mooo-vies!

Q: What does a spider's bride wear?

A: A webbing dress!

Q: What is the smartest creature on earth?

A: A spelling bee

Q: How did the preschoolers learn how to make banana splits?

A: They went to sundae school!

Q: What is the absolute worst thing about throwing a party in space?

A: You have to plan it!

Q: Why did the policeman go to the baseball game?
A: Because he overheard someone had stolen a base so he went to check it out!

Q: Two pairs of pant are worn by golfers at the tournament. What is the reason for this?
A: It was in case they got a hole in one!

Q: What sort of shoes do robbers wear?
A: Sneak-ers!

Q: What do you call two guys hanging out on a curtain?
A: Curt and Rod

Q: Why was the Math book so sad?
A: It was dealing with too many problems!

Q: What time would it be when Godzilla came to hang out?
A: Time to run!

Q: Why did the dog do so well in school?
A: Because he was the teacher's pet!

Q: Why did the egg get thrown out of class?

A: Because he wouldn't stop telling yolks!

Q: What did one penny say to the other while having a conversation?

A: We make perfect cents!

Q: What is the reason behind arresting the belt?

A: Because some pants were being held up by it!

Q: Why did the computer go to the hospital?

A: It became sick with a virus!

Q: Where does the president keep his armies?

A: In his sleeves!

Q: What remark did one firefly receive from the other?

A: You're glowing, girl!

Q: Why did the cucumber blush?

A: He saw the salad dressing!

Q: What do you call a blind dinosaur?

A: Do-you-think-he-saw-us!

Q: How do you catch an entire school of fish?

A: With bookworms!

Q: Why did the mushroom like to party so much?

A: Because he was fungi!

Q: What do you call a guy lying on the front porch?

A: Matt

Q: What do snowmen call their annual ball?

A: The snowball!

Q: If you've seen a spaceman, what will you do?

A: I will be parking my car.

Q: What do cows read?

A: Cattle-logs

Q: Where do young cows eat lunch?

A: In the calf-ateria!

Q: What did the policeman say to his stomach?

A: Stop! You are under a vest!

Q: What do birds give out in their Christmas stockings?

A: Tweets!

Q: How do mountains stay warm in the winter?

A: Snowcaps!

Q: How did the calendar become well-liked?

A: Because he went on so many dates!

Q: What is the reason why the broom is not always on time?

A: It over swept!

Q: Near the sea is where seagulls prefer to live. What is the reason behind this?

A: They will be bagels if they will live by the bay?

Q: After tripping and falling over, what did the horse exclaimed?

A: I fell and can't giddy up!

Q: The girl volcano heard this from the boy volcano. What is it?

A: I lava you!

Q: Name the kind of car that is driven by the girlfriend of Mickey Mouse.

A: A Minnie-van

Q: When you see a sick bird, what will you give it?

A: A special tweetment!

Q: Fishes are wise. Why is that?
A: Because they are always in schools!

Q: What animal has more lives than a cat?
A: A frog. They croak every night!

Q: What musical instrument is always in the bathroom next to the sink?
A: A tuba toothpaste!

Q: Where do pencils take vacations?
A: Pencil-vania!

Q: What kind of music do rabbits and frogs like the best?
A: Hip-hop!

Q: Eight heard this from zero. What is it?
A: Nice belt!

Q: The neck scarf heard this from the snowcap. What is it?
A: Hey, neck scarf, hang around. I will go up ahead.

Q: What time of day do ducks wake up?

A: They wake up at the quack of dawn!

Q: What does the lion say when he first meets another animal in the jungle?
A: Hi, I'm a lion. Pleased to eat you!

Q: What types of markets do dogs and cats hate?
A: Flea-markets!

Q: What do you call a bear that is slowly losing its teeth?
A: You call it a gummy bear.

Q: What do you call a pig that practices martial arts?
A: A porkchop

Q: When a cow is caught in a tornado, what do you call it?
A: A milkshake

Q: When you see a sleeping bull, what do you call it?
A: A bulldozer

Q: Tell me the difference between climate and weather.
A: You are able to climb it but you cannot weather a tree.

Q: What does the tree wear to the summer pool parties?

A: Swimming trunks!

Q: Why did the sun go to school?
A: To get brighter!

Q: How does a ghost stay safe when he is driving?
A: He puts on his sheet belt!

Q: What do monsters turn on in the summer time?
A: Their scare conditioner!

Q: What is scarecrows' favorite food?
A: Strawberries!

Q: What kind of monster loves the disco?
A: The boogieman!

Q: Why do witches always say their name when they start a conversation?
A: So they know which witch is which!

Q: How do you make a witch itch?
A: Take away the 'W'

Q: Why is it always safe to tell a mummy your secrets?

A: Because they will keep it under wraps!

Q: Which of Santa's reindeer has an attitude problem?
A: Rude-olph!

Q: What is Frosty the Snowman's favorite type of cereal?
A: Frosted Flakes

Q: What did the hamburger name her daughter when she was born?
A: Patty!

Q: Where does Superman like to shop for food?
A: At the supermarket!

Q: A cow that has no legs is called?
A: Ground beef!

Q: What did the skeleton order for dinner?
A: Spare ribs!

Q: What is a balloon's least favorite kind of music?
A: Pop music!

Q: Why did the musician get arrested?
A: He got into some treble!

Q: What is a skeleton's favorite instrument?

A: A trombone!

Q: Which punk rock group has four men who can't sing to save their lives?

A: Mount Rushmore!

Q: What sorts of tunes do the planets listen to?

A: Nep-tunes!

Q: A bear that weighs 6,000 pounds should go where?

A: It should go dieting!

Q: Where did two walls meet?

A: On the corner!

Q: Why does a dragon always sleep from 8:00 am to 4:00 pm?

A: So they can fight knights!

Q: Cards cannot be played by pirates. Why is that?

A: Because all over the deck he walks!

Q: Two elevators are talking to each other. What did they say to each other?

A: I am not feeling good. I feel like something is coming down with me.

Q: How is a headache cured?
A: The pane will disappear if you put your head through a window!

Q: Before robbing the bank, the robber took a bath. Why is that?
A: He wants to have a clean get-a-way!

Q: What did two pencils tell one another?
A: You are looking kinda dull. Are you okay?!

Q: Why are frogs always in such a good mood?
A: They just eat whatever bugs them!

Q: What sound do porcupines make when they smooch?
A: Ouch!

Q: What did the blanket say to comfort the bed when he was upset?
A: Don't worry! I got you covered!

Q: This contains thousands of letters, ends in letter E, and begins with letter P. What do you call it?
A: A post office!

Chapter 4: Longer Dumb Jokes

George was on his way home from a party. He was walking down the street when he heard something behind him. It was making a booming noise. BOOM! BOOM! BOOM! He turned around to see a coffin following him! He started running to his house. The coffin kept following him. It got louder and louder! BOOM! BOOM! BOOM! George was frightened. Once he reached the front door of his house, he noticed the coffin right behind him. He quickly unlocked the door and tried to push the coffin out, but it followed him in any way. He ran upstairs to his bedroom and grabbed the first thing he could to throw at the coffin. A bag of cough drops. He threw them, and the coffin stopped.

"Oh no!" the kangaroo said to the snake. "We are supposed to get some rain today!"
"What is wrong with that?" said the snake. "We could use some rain. It's so dry here!"
"It just means my kids are going to have to play inside all day!" groaned the kangaroo.

A woman asked her lawyer about his fees. He told her he charges $100 for every three questions. The woman said that seems like a bit much, don't you think? He replied yes but those are my charges. He asked her what her final question was.

A little girl is sitting at home and hears a knock at the front door. She opens it and screams in disgust. It was a turtle. She throws it as far as she can and shuts the door. A year later, she hears a knock at the door. She opens it and sees a turtle. He asks, "What was that all about?"

A snail went to a car dealership. The salesman was very surprised that the snail wanted to buy a fast, sportscar. When the snail requested to have the sides of the car painted with a big 'S', the salesman was surprised even more. He asked the snail why he would want something like that. The snail replied, "I want people to say, 'look at that S car go!'"

Three men are driving through the desert when their car breaks down. They each bring an item to take on their hike into town. One of the men grabs a jug of water. The second one takes a box of crackers. The third takes the car door. One of the men says that they can drink the water in case they get thirsty. The other says they can eat the crackers in case they get hungry. The third one says he can roll down the window in case they get hot.

A father and daughter walk into a library. They both look at each other and ask the front desk clerk for two cheeseburgers and two orders of fries. The librarian looks at them and tells them they are in a library. The man says 'Oh' and whispers to the librarian, "We will take two cheeseburgers and two orders of fries."

A small chicken walks into a library and says, "Book, book, book!" The librarian hands the chicken a couple of small paperback books and watches as the chicken leaves the library. He walks across the street, over a hill, and disappears from the librarian's sight.
The next day the same chicken comes into the library and says, "Book, book, book!" The librarian does the same thing. She hands the chicken a few small, paperback books and watches the chicken cross the road and go over the hill. The chicken disappears from her sight again.
The day after that, the chicken walks back into the library and says, "Book, book, book!" She hands the chicken the books but instead of watching the chicken disappear, she follows it. They both cross the street and go over the hill. When they get to the other side of the hill, the librarian watches as the chicken walks up to the biggest frog she has ever seen. The chicken hands the books to the frog and he says, "Read it…read it…read it."

A son and father were sitting down for dinner. The boy turns to his dad and asks, "Dad, are bugs good to eat?"

The dad turns to his son and tells him, "Don't talk about stuff like that at dinner. That is inappropriate while we are eating!"
After the two are done eating dinner, the dad asks his son why he would ask such a question. The boy looks at his father and says, "Well, there was a big bug in your soup, but it's gone now."

Teacher: "If I gave you three cats, plus another two cats, and then another one cat. How many would you have?"
Boy: "Seven."
Teacher: "No, listen carefully. If I gave you three cats, plus two more cats, plus another cat, how many would you have?"
Boy: "Seven."
Teacher: "Okay, let me put this in a different way. If I gave you three oranges, plus two more oranges, and another one orange, how many would you have?
Boy: "Six."
Teacher: "Okay. So, if you have three cats, and I gave you two more, plus one more, how many would you have?"
Boy: "Seven."
Teacher: "No, where are you getting the number seven from?"
Boy: "I already have a cat at home!"

Mr. and Mrs. Shoe had two sons. One was named Mind Your Own Business and the other was named Trouble. The two sons decided to play a game of hide-and-seek. Trouble went to go hide while Mind

Your Own Business counted down from one hundred. Mind Your Own Business started searching for his brother everywhere. He looked underneath cars. He looked in bushes and around in a dark alley near their house. A police officer walked up to him and asked him what he was doing. "I'm playing a game," replied the brother. The policeman asked him what his name was to which the boy replied, "Mind Your Own Business." The police officer grew angry. He said, "Listen, son. Are you looking for Trouble?" Mind Your Own Business replied, "Yes. Actually, I am."

A teacher asks her students to make a sentence using the word 'beans'. One small girl spoke up and said, "My mom cooks beans at home." Another little girl stood up and said, "My father grows his own beans in our garden." A third little girl stood up and said, "We are all human beans."

A robber goes into a bank and holds everyone hostage. He says, "Give me all of your money or your chemistry!" One of the bank tellers says, "Don't you mean history?" The robber tells the bank teller, "Don't change the subject!"

Him: "Oh, no! I just fell off a 50ft ladder!"
Her: "Oh, wow! Are you okay?"
Him: "Yeah, I fell off of the first step."

One night, a queen and a king went into the castle. There was no one in the castle and no one ever came out of it. The next morning, three people walked out of the castle. Who were they? The knight, the queen, and the king.

A man was driving down the road when a policeman stopped him. When the officer approached the car, he asked the man why he had penguins in the backseat? The man replied, "These are my penguins. They belong to me." The officer said that the man needs to take them to the zoo. The next day, the police officer saw the same man driving down the road. He pulled him over to make sure he had taken the penguins to the zoo. This time, when he saw the man and the penguins, they all had sunglasses on. The police officer told him, "I thought I told you to take these penguins to the zoo?" He then replied, "I did! Today we are going to the beach!"

One person decided to pay his buddy a visit. When he arrived at his house, his mouth dropped. A dog and his friend were focused on a game of chess. The man said, "That is amazing! This has to be the smartest dog in the entire world." His friend replied. "No, not really. I've won the last three out of five games!"

A spell was put over a prince. He is only allowed to speak just a word every year. He can speak two words in a year if he doesn't speak a word the previous year, and so forth. He then met a pretty woman one day. In order for him to tell her, "my dear," he decided to not speak to her for two years. He also wants her to know that he loves her. So, before he could say anything to her, he needs to wait again for three years. After five years, he wants to ask her to marry him. So, he still needs to wait for four more years. At last, after nine years, the man can finally say, "My dear, I love you. Will you marry me?" The beautiful woman said, "I'm sorry. I didn't hear you. What?"

Connor went to go visit his 90-year old grandpa who lived far out in the country. He was going to stay for a couple of days. The first morning, his grandpa made Connor a plate full of bacon and eggs. Connor felt a weird film on the plate. He asked his grandpa if the plate was clean. His grandpa replied, "They are as clean as Cold Water can get them!" The next morning, Connor's grandpa made toast and sausage. Connor saw some left-over egg on the plate. He asked his grandpa if the plates were clean and his grandpa assured him they were. He said, "They are as clean as Cold Water can get them."

Connor was getting ready to leave his grandpa's house. When he was on his way to the front door, his grandpa's dog stopped him and began growling. Connor yelled at his grandpa, "Grandpa! Your dog won't let me leave!" His grandpa yells back, "Cold Water, go lie down! Let Connor leave."

Four men are waiting in a hospital lobby while their wives are having babies. The first nurse comes out of the room and yells at the first man. "Congratulations, you have twins!"

The man replies, "That's funny. I work for the Minnesota Twins!"

The second nurse comes out of the room and yells at the second man.

"Congratulations, you have triplets!"

The second man replies, "That's funny. I work for the 3M Company!"

The third nurse comes out of the room and yells at the third man.

"Congratulations, you have quadruplets!"

The third man replies, "That's funny. I work for The Four Seasons hotel."

The last man begins crying. All of the other men look at him and ask him what is wrong.

"The last man replies, "I work for 7-Up."

The teacher asked little Bobby if he knew his numbers. He replied yes.

"Good!" the teacher says. "What comes after four?"

"Five," says Bobby.

"What about after seven?" replies the teacher.

"Eight," says Bobby.

"How about after nine?" says the teacher.

"Ten," says Bobby with a loud sigh. Bobby was growing bored of the teacher's questions.

"Okay then. What about after ten?" says the teacher.

"Jack," says Bobby.

A man comes home after a long day of work. He opens the fridge to get out a nice, cold soda. Inside, he sees a rabbit taking a little nap. The man carefully wakes up the rabbit.

He asks, "What are you doing in my fridge?"

The rabbit replies, "Isn't this a Westinghouse?"

"Uh, yes," the man replies. "It is."

"Well then," the rabbit replies, "I'm twying to west."

A businessman walked into work one morning to find that some handymen were repainting the building. He noticed that they were all wearing two windbreakers. The businessman found it a bit strange because it was a hot summer's day.

It bothered the businessman so much that he finally left his office and went to ask the handymen why they were wearing two windbreakers.

One of the handymen replied, "The can says, for best results, please use two coats."

A huge cruise ship passes by a small island. All of the passengers see a bearded man on the island running around and flailing his arms.

"Captain," one of the passengers asks, "who is that man over there on the island?"

"I have no idea," the captain replies, "but every time we drive by here, he goes crazy!"

One day, a man walks into the movie theatre with an elephant.

"I'm sorry, sir. I can't allow you to bring in an elephant to the movie theatre," says one of the managers.

"Oh, he is well-behaved! I promise," says the man.

"All right then. If you are one-hundred percent sure," says the manager.

After the movie, the manager walks up to the man. "I'm so surprised. Your elephant was so well-behaved!"

The man says, "I am, too. He hated the book!"

A small boy walked into a restaurant. He saw a sign outside that said fat-free French fries. He thought to himself that they sounded great and he was starving!

"I'll take an order of fat-free French fries," says the boy to the older gentlemen behind the counter.

"Okay, coming right up!" says the older man.

A basket of French fries was being watched by the boy as it was taken out from the fryer by the cook. When the cook placed the potatoes in a box for to-go, oil was still dripping from them.

"Hang on for a second," said the boy. "Those fries don't look fat-free."

"Sure they are," said the man. "We only charge for the potatoes. The fat is completely free."

Two dogs, a Chihuahua and a Dalmatian, were being walked by two friends. Suddenly, when they were near a restaurant, they smelled something amazing coming from it.

The man who owns the Dalmatian asks the other guy if he wants to get something to eat.

"Sure," he says, "but we have dogs with us. They won't let us in."

The guy with the Dalmatian says, "Follow my lead." After putting on a pair of sunglasses, he walked into the restaurant.

'I'm sorry, sir. You can't bring your dog in here," says the manager. "We have a strict no pets policy."

"This is my seeing-eye dog," says the man with the Dalmatian.

"A Dalmatian?" says the manager, confused.

"Yes, they are using Dalmatians now," says the man.

"Very well, then. Come on in," says the manager.

The guy with the Chihuahua follows his friends lead. He puts on some sunglasses and then walked over inside the restaurant.

The manager says, "Sorry, sir. No pets allowed."

The guy says, "but this is my seeing-eye dog."

"A Chihuahua?" says the manager.

"A Chihuahua?!" says the man. "They gave me a Chihuahua?"

Chapter 5: Kids' Puns and Other Jokes

Have you heard about the man that has his entire left side cut off? He is all right now.

My leaf blower just doesn't blow. Man, it sucks.

I'm great friends with twenty-five letters of the alphabet. I don't know why.

Somehow, I have forgotten which side the sun has risen when I woke up this morning. Suddenly, it dawned on me.

A golf ball is always going to be a golf ball. It doesn't matter how you putt it.

Can your dog do magic tricks? Mine can. He's a labracadabrador.

I tried to capture some fog. I mist.

The longer you sleep in a bed, the taller you are.

There was a boomerang joke I heard earlier, and it was really funny. I can't remember it, though. Give me a minute. It'll come back to me.

Some whiteboards are simply remarkable.

What would be the point in the end if you can make both ends of a pencil as erasers?

I was figuring out how lightning is formed as I watched a thunderstorm. Suddenly, it struck me!

A little word of advice. You should never lie to an x-ray technician. They'll always be able to see right through you.

Speed bumps are what I am extremely scared of. You shouldn't worry though. I'll get over it slowly.

I read a sales advertisement that says, "TV for sale, $1, volume stuck on full." I cannot turn that down, I thought.

Wow! That wedding was so emotional. The cake was in tiers.

Broken puppets for sale. No strings attached!

I couldn't have time to search for my lost watch.

Dead batteries were being sold on a shop I happened to pass by. There was absolutely no charge!

A long time ago, I was a soap-addict. Fortunately, I am now cleaned.

The other day, I was walking behind a clown. We both walked into the same shopping store and he opened the door for me. I thought to myself. Man, what a good jester.

The person who invented the knock-knock joke was a genius! Give that guy a no-bell prize!

I used to sing in the shower. It was great fun until I got soap in my mouth. I asked my mom how to stop it from happening. She said stop singing those soap operas.

I would like to make you laugh with my joke about construction, but I forgot the punch line. I am still working on it.

The newly bought stair lift was giving my grandma a lot of problems. It literally drives her up a wall.

I have a gift for the guy who invented the zero. Nothing!

A camouflage shirt is what I really wanted to buy. However, the right one cannot be found.

There are new reversible jackets that recently came out. Have you heard about them? How good they will turn out is a mystery.

I was figuring out how my seatbelt should be properly fastened, but it didn't work. Then it clicked!

A man just assaulted that lady with cow's milk, cheese, and some butter! How dairy!

I didn't know how I felt after my mood ring was stolen by someone.

Some food coloring was what I accidentally swallowed yesterday. When I went to the doctor, he said I was fine. I felt like I dyed a little inside.

I wondered why the baseball got bigger and bigger. And then it hit me!

Some guy was hit by a soda bottle in the head. Luckily, it was a soft drink.

These stairs cannot be trusted. They are always up to no good!

Again, my printer's making some music. I think the paper's jamming.

I saw a snake next to a Lego set the other day. I think he was a boa constructor.

My time machine and I go waaayyyy back!

The drill is known by the dentist's regular visitors.

Since she's always counting, I no longer hang out with my ex-best friend. I wonder what she is up to now!

My sister could not believe that I could make a new car made of noodles, so she made a bet of $100. The look on her face when I rode pasta was satisfying.

I have to put my foot down, finally, when I was told to stop acting a flamingo by my mom.

I have to blame my shelf when a book fell on my head.

A new type of broom came out today. People were standing in line waiting to buy it. It's really sweeping the nation!

My girlfriend quit her job at the donut factory. She was so sick and tired of the hole business.

A boiled egg in the morning is sure hard to beat.

Did you hear about the old Italian waiter? He pasta way last week.

Learning how to collect trash was difficult. I just picked it up as I went on.

My dog loves pizza. His favorite is puperoni.

Children who fail their coloring tests always need a shoulder to crayon.

The spider had to use the computer. He needed to check on his web site.

The Energizer Bunny was arrested. He was charged with battery.

"Doctor, there is a patient on line one who says he is invisible."
"Well, tell him I cannot see him right now."

I was addicted to the Hokey Pokey. Luckily, I turned myself around.

I was grateful that you explained to me the word 'many.' It means a lot.

I accidentally handed my best friend a glue stick instead of Chapstick. Now, he's not talking to me.

How did I get fired from the calendar factory, you may ask? Well, I just wanted to take a day off!

Just don't spell part backward. Trust me, it's a trap!

Did you watch the news? There was a kidnapping at the middle school. Everything is okay, though. He woke up.

A friend of mine tried to annoy me with bird buns, but I realized toucan play that game.

The bike was two-tired to stand up on its own.

If a baby refuses to sleep during nap-time, are they resisting a rest?

Chapter 6: Quirky Questions

Why does the feet smell and nose run?

If it is only happening in North America, then why do they call it The World Series?

Why is it called a building if it is already built?

If practice makes perfect, and nobody is perfect, why should they have to practice?

If a tomato is a fruit, is ketchup a smoothie?

Why is the glue not sticking inside the bottle of the glue?

If number two pencils are the most popular type of pencil, why are they called number twos?

Would seven days without exercise make one weak?

Why do you call it 'rush hour' when the traffic is slow?

Why does our hair lighten and our skin darkens when exposed to the sun?

Why does the watch's third hand call the second hand?

How much deeper would the ocean be without sponges?

How do 'stay off the grass' signs get there in the first place?

Why is it called the Secret Service if everyone knows about it?

If a mime is arrested, do the police have to tell him that he has the right to remain silent?

Why is it called a television set if you only get one TV?

Why do pizza shops put round pizzas into square boxes?

Why apartments are always built together?

Why do we drive on parkways and park in driveways?

Why is mail that gets delivered by the sea called 'CARgo' but mail delivered on land is called 'SHIPments?'

Chapter 7: Books Never Written

"How to fish" by Will Ketchum

"Healthy Foods" by Chris P. Bacon

"Living through the Storms" by Ty Foon

"Musical Instruments" by ZylaFone

"Starting a Fire" by M. Burr

"How to Win a 5k Marathon" by Sprintz A. Lott

"Architecture" by Bill Dhing

"Flying Beasts" by Tara Dactle

"Answering the Door" by Isabelle Rings

"Batman's Worst Enemy" by Joe Kurr

"Learning to Read" by Abe E. Seas

"A Guide to Flying" by Al T. Tude

"Dessert" by Sue Flay

"A Guide to New York" by Dee Big Apple

"A Detective's Case" by Mr. E.

"A Butterfly's Life" by Kat E. Pillar

"Giant Snakes" by Ann A. Conda

"How to Wrestle Bears" by Dan Jerus

"How to Work Out" by Jim Nasium

"Mathematics" by Jean Yuss

"How to be Helpful" by Linda Hand

"A Day at the Beach" by Sandy Feat

"Woodwind Instruments" by Clair E. Nett

"Everything is Going Wrong" by Mel Function

"To the Outhouse" by Willy Mayket; illustrated by Bettee Wont

"Walking to School" by Misty Bus

"Where have all of the Animals Gone?" by Darin DeBarn

"Falling off of a Cliff" by Aileen Dover N. Fell

"I was Prepared" by Justine Kase

"Green Spots on the Walls" by Picken and Flicken

"The Lost Scout" by Werram Eye

'The Bearded Man" by Harry Chin

"Crossing a Man with a Duck" by Willie Waddle

"Raise Your Arms" by Harry Pitts

"Sitting on the Beach" by Sandi C. Heeks

"My Life as a Gas Station Attendant" by Phil R. Awp

"Something Smells" by I Ben Phartin

"Household Book of Tools" by M.C. Hammer

"Late for Work" by Dr. Wages

"Computer Memory" by Meg. A. Byte

"The Future of Robotics" by Ann Droid and Cy B. Org

"What to do if you are in a Car Accident" by Rhea Ender

"Taking Tests" by B. A. Wiseman

"Over the Mountaintop" by Hugo First

Conclusion

Thank you for making through to the end of *Karen's OMG Joke Book for Kids: Funny, Silly, Dumb Jokes that Will Make Children Roll on the Floor Laughing.* Let's hope it was filled with the necessary information to make your child laugh!

This book has been written for younger kids. It isn't just the normal knock-knock jokes, although they are in the book. This book is filled with all sorts of jokes that will surely get your child laughing! There are some that will make them think. Some of them are just really bad puns that will make, even you, shake your head. There are also some classic riddles that are so popular that they've withstood the test of time. You can enjoy it as a family or leave your child to use their imagination. The book is free of dirty jokes and all jokes that use profanity. I hope you enjoyed it!

Connect with us on our Facebook page www.facebook.com/bluesourceandfriends and stay tuned to our latest book promotions and free giveaways.

Karen's Dad Jokes

The Bad, The Funny, The Clean, And the LOL Jokes For The Cool Dad

Karen J. Bun

Table of Contents

Description

Discover the silly, clean, Laugh Out Loud jokes dad loves to tell again and again. Some of the jokes here will seem redundant, but they are all uniquely resonant to Dad who loves a good pun. Dad is a cool guy no matter what, right? We all know Dad will never pass up the opportunity to tell a corny yet funny joke. It is in their blood. They cannot help it at all. Dads will be dads, and they will always want to make us, and everyone else, laugh. This book is a celebration of dads and their innate humor. The guy who is so cool he can tell the silliest joke while appearing equally confident and in charge. It might be cheesy, but if you've ever had a dad who liked to crack a good, terrible, joke, you will appreciate all of the inclusions here.

Dad with his one-liners, what he thinks to be a clever play on words, and groan-inducing, hand-hitting-the-face hilarity, will never think to not share what he deems a funny joke. He won't just share it quietly nor elegantly either. Dad will make every effort to entice us into his provocations while thinking they are completely normal and genuinely funny. I think dad would definitely approve of the jokes here.

Some are tried and tested while others are modern and cool. This book would make a perfect Father's Day gift, birthday gift, holiday, or any special occasion to celebrate Dad gift! These are a few of the silly, banal, absurd, ridiculous, and plain old funny jokes you will read that we have all heard dad say one time or another:

- Discover new, funny animal jokes along with the classics
- Silly jokes about everyday matters, people, family, and things
- Hilarious occupation jokes
- Bad, cheesy, corny, repetitive jokes we all know, but hearing dad say them, just makes them all funnier
- Clean but funny weather and nature jokes
- Jokes and puns about famous people and events
- Laugh Out Loud sports jokes
- Downright silly book titles and authors
- Absurd holiday jokes to make you chuckle

Bluesource And Friends

This book is brought to you by Bluesource And Friends, a happy book publishing company.

Our motto is **"Happiness Within Pages."**

We promise to deliver amazing value to readers with our books.

We also appreciate honest book reviews from our readers.

Connect with us on our Facebook page www.facebook.com/bluesourceandfriends and stay tuned to our latest book promotions and free giveaways.

Don't forget to claim your FREE book

https://tinyurl.com/karenbrainteasers

Also check out our best seller book

https://tinyurl.com/lateralthinkingpuzzles

Introduction

Congratulations on downloading your copy of *Karen's Dad Jokes: The Bad, the Funny, the Clean, and the LOL Jokes for the Cool Dad*. I am so glad you have decided to explore funny dad jokes for all to enjoy, young and old. Some of us may know for certain that dads and jokes go hand-in-hand. It's inevitable. Dads pretty much just have to tell jokes as soon as they officially become Dad. It is second nature; it is in their DNA. If there wasn't a dad out there who could make us laugh, chuckle, groan out loud, or shake our heads at the hilarious absurdity, then we would all be missing out. Life would not be the same without a good, bad, witty one-liner or corny jibe courtesy of good ol' dad.

Dads enjoy a cheeky pun, play on words, trite tale, or tall story or two, or three, or four. I think it must be irresistible for any dad to pass a practical joke or funny story as his own. If there is a chance to always repeat a cheesy gag or funny joke of the day, then dad is going to shine and perform the best way he knows how. His kids, co-workers, students, family, and friends may be completely embarrassed or falling over with laughter, but dad cannot and will not resist a good, silly, corny joke, especially at the expense of others. Dads themselves will admit they cannot help themselves when it comes to telling an irresistibly bad joke or pun. Everyone listening in the room can moan and roll their eyes, but dad will have the biggest grin on his face, satisfied he told yet another, really bad, joke.

This book is for the entire family to enjoy and refer to over and over again. You will find classic laughs and puns about all kinds of animals, famous people and events, nature, sports, occupations, school jokes, and more. Let dad know you appreciate him and his remarkable timing and wit by sharing these jokes with him. This book is for the young, the old, and the funny Dad of all ages!

work or a recorded copy and is only allowed with an expressed written consent from the Publisher. All additional rights reserved.

The information in the following pages is broadly considered to be a truthful and accurate account of facts and as such any inattention, use, or misuse of the information in question by the reader will render any resulting actions solely under their purview. There are no scenarios in which the publisher or the original author of this work can be in any fashion deemed liable for any hardship or damages that may befall them after undertaking information described herein.

Additionally, the information in the following pages is intended only for informational purposes and should thus be thought of as universal. As befitting its nature, it is presented without assurance regarding its prolonged validity or interim quality. Trademarks that are mentioned are done without written consent and can in no way be considered an endorsement from the trademark holder.

Animal Jokes

Q: Did you hear about the paranoid bloodhound?

A: He thought everyone was following him!

Q: Where is the best place in the house to keep sled dogs?

A: In a mush room.

Q: Which dinosaur had radial wheels?

A: Tire-rannosaurus Rex.

Q: When a dog suddenly sat on sandpaper, what did it say?

A: Ruff.

Q: Phones and dogs are alike. Why?

A: Collar IDs make them both the same.

Q: When it's raining dogs and cats, what happens?

A: Stepping in a poodle is a possibility.

Q: Dogs are surely not good dancers, why?

A: Having 2 left feet is the reason why.

Q: The best time is kept by what kind of dog?

A: A watch dog.

Q: The poor dog chases his own tail. Why?

A: He wants to try to make both ends meet!

Q: Bubble baths are loved by what kind of dog?

A: It's called a shampoodoodle.

Q: A left-handed dog is called?

A: A south paw!

Q: Two fleas are talking to each other. What are they talking about?

A: Are we taking or walking a dog?

Q: The legs of a horse should be how long?

A: The ground must be reached by the horse. That's how long they should be.

Q: This type of markets is avoided by dogs. What is it?

A: Flea markets!

Q: When the cowboy's dog ran away, what did he say?

A: Well, doggone!

Q: This state has many dogs and cats. What is it?
A: Petsylvania

Q: Have you heard about the sea lions that perform?
A: I heard their reviews are wave!

Q: What is the name of the first cat that has flown an airplane?
A: Kitty-hawk

Q: The dinosaur couldn't walk, why?
A: Because it was extinct.

Q: What did Mr. Fox say when he tucked his children into bed?
A: Please have pheasant dreams.

Customer: Is that dog a good watchdog?
Pet store owner: Of course. He'll cause a ruckus every time he sees a stranger!
Customer: How do I know you are not just making that up?
Pet store owner: Because the dog comes with a money bark guarantee!

Mr. Beaver: I'm so hungry. What is for dinner?
Mrs. Beaver: A tree course meal.

Q: What's the reason the man is standing behind the horse?

A: Getting a kick out of it was what he was hoping for.

Q: Hair can be seen mostly on which horse's side?

A: The outside.

Q: A horse is scared of getting this disease. What is it?

A: Hay fever.

Q: What is the only time that a horse talks?

A: Whinney wants to!

Q: A horse that is living next door is called?

A: A neigh-bor.

Q: When the horse entered the class, what did the teacher said?

A: What's with the long face?

Q: A horse fell. What did he exclaim?

A: I couldn't giddyup after falling.

Q: A pony gargles because…?

A: It's a bit hoarse!

Q: A horse can be led to the water in this way. What is it?

A: With a lot of oats, carrots, and apples

Q: It was Friday when a man rode his horse. He, then, rode on Friday the next day. How did that happen?

A: Friday was the name of the horse.

Q: What did the hungry spider say to the other spider at the end of the week?

A: Thank goodness, it is Flyday!

Q: Why did the little girl love those talking birds so much?

A: She loved them so much because they were her grand parrots.

Q: Have you ever seen a catfish?

A: No. How did he hold the reel and rod?

Q: Why did the King of Beasts wear a cowboy hat and cowboy boots?

A: Because he wanted to do some country lion dancing.

Q: What is the reason behind the cat going to medical school?

A: He dreams of becoming a first aid kit.

Q: When going for a field trip, what is the preferred place by school kittens?
A: To the mewseum

Q: This is the best game that the cat likes playing with the mouse.
A: Catch!

Q: The song that is liked the most by a cat is?
A: Three Blind Mice.

Q: A leopard cannot hide because?
A: Because he's always spotted!

Q: Cats are good when it comes to video games. Why?
A: Having nine lives is the reason.

Q: A Red Cross-working kitten is called?
A: A first-aid Kit

Q: There is something worse than raining dogs and cats. What is it?
A: Hailing taxi cabs!

Q: The favorite color of the cat is?
A: Purrr-ple

Q: Why didn't the shark have to pay cash at the grocery store?

A: He had a credit cod with him.

Q: Why was Mrs. Rabbit so upset when I saw her earlier today?

A: Mrs. Rabbit was having a very bad hare day.

It's raining dogs and cats outside!

Yes, it is raining dogs and cats outside. I must have stepped in a hundred poodles.

Q: Why are elephants no longer allowed to swim in public swimming pools?

A: Elephants are banned from public swimming pools because they kept dropping their trunks.

Q: A charging bear can be stopped. How?

A: His credits cards should be taken away.

Q: What can adult cats have that no other creature can have?

A: Kittens

Mrs. Rabbit: How can I stay cool in the summer?

Mr. Bunny: You can always buy a good hare conditioner.

Q: What does the littlest duck in the family wear?

A: It will always wear the hand me down.

Q: What happens when fifty rabbits hop backward at the same time?

A: You get a receding hare line.

Q: What is white and black and white and black purple?

A: A violet has been stuck on the hoof of a zebra and its rolling down the hill.

Q: Differentiate a comma and a cat.

A: The end of the paws of a cat has its claws, while the end of a clause of a comma has a pause.

Q: Why did the minnow now want to go to lunch with the stork?

A: He was afraid he would get stuck with the bill.

Q: Why do lobsters not like to share?

A: Lobsters are always shellfish.

Q: Why do kangaroos make for really bad sailors?

A: Because kangaroos always jump ship.

Mr. Cockroach: Mrs. Centipede, why do you look so sad?

Mrs. Centipede: I have ten children and school starts tomorrow.

Mr. Cockroach: Most parents are excited when school starts again.

Mrs. Cockroach: Not me. All my children need new shoes!

Q: Why did the guppy join the Army's motorized vehicle division?

A: The guppy just wanted to be in a fish tank.

Classroom and Kids' Jokes

Q: Geometry teachers like what kind of lunch?

A: Square meals.

Q: 5 and 6 are scared of 7. Why?

A: Because seven ate nine.

Student: Ma'am, if there is something that I didn't do, would you be mad at me?

Teacher: No, of course!

Student: I didn't do my assignment.

Q: The mathematics book is always so sad. What do you think is the reason?

A: The reason is the many problems he has.

Q: How do you like Kindergarten, Billy?

A: I can't do anything there. I don't like it.

Q: What do you mean you can't do anything?

A: Reading and writing are foreign to me. And yet, they don't allow talking.

Q: The biology teacher didn't get married to the physics teacher because of this reason. What is it?

A: The chemistry between the two of them isn't right.

Student: My dog tried to chew up my essay homework last night.

Teacher: What did you do?

Student: I took the words right out of his mouth.

Q: Why would you bring a jump rope to school?

A: So that you can ask the principal if you can skip a grade.

Q: Who calculates how many meals are served in the cafeteria?

A: The lunch counter.

Q: Why did they evacuate the school library?

A: Because someone found dynamite in the dictionary.

Student #1: What is the difference between snow and snew?

Student #2: What's snew?

Student #1: I don't know. What's new with you?

Q: The math classroom's windowsill has a plant sitting on it. What happened to it?

A: Square roots grew from it.

Q: Where do people who play piano go to be on vacation?

A: Pianists go to the Florida Keys to be on vacation.

Q: Name the state in the entire America that is considered to be the wisest.

A: Having four As and a single B makes Alabama the smartest.

Q: It can travel all over the world despite staying in just one corner. What is it?

A: A stamp.

Teacher: What state do pencils originate from?

Student: Why, Pennsylvania, of course.

Teacher: Can you please tell me the name of the Great Plains?

Student: Sure, the F-16, Concorde, and 747.

Teacher: Where can you find the English Channel?

Student: I don't have that on my TV, so I do not know!

Q: Name the world's quickest and fastest country.

A: The fastest country in the world is Russia.

Q: Della wore this clothing. What is it?

A: Her New Jersey

Q: Washington's capital is?
A: The W!

Q: In an exam, what city cheats?
A: The cheating city is Peking

Q: What rock group has four main men but men who do not sing at all?
A: Mount Rushmore

Teacher: Do you know anything about the Dead Sea?
Student: Did it die because of sickness?

Q: What did the earthquake hear from the ground?
A: The ground said, "You crack me up!"

Q: Why is the ladder needed by the music teacher?
A: So the teacher could reach all the high notes.

Q: College isn't needed by the sun. Why?
A: Having a million degrees is the reason why.

Q: The cafeteria's clock is slow. Why?
A: It always went back four seconds.

Q: Librarians like these vegetables. What are they?

A: Quiet peas.

Q: Librarians take them when they are fishing. What are they?

A: Bookworms

Q: Name the tallest building in the world.

A: Library. It has many stories.

Q: This happened due to the invention of the wheel. What is it?

A: A revolution has happened.

Q: Can you guess how the hair of the moon was cut by the barber?

A: E-clipse it!

Q: This is what the pencil heard from the pencil sharpener. What is it?

A: Get to the point! Stop going in circles!

Q: What time do astronauts have their meals?

A: At launch time!

Q: This is considered to be the classroom's king. What object is it?

A: The ruler!

Q: This keeps the sun in the sky. What is it?

A: Sunbeams!

Q: So, how's school? Have you learned something today?

A: I still haven't learned enough. I still need to go tomorrow.

Q: This is what is taught to the elves in their school.

A: The elf-abet!

Q: The kid studied while on an airplane. Why is that?

A: Having a higher education is what he wanted.

Q: Guess what the pen said to the pencil.

A: And your point is?

Q: Getting straight A's can be easily done by…?

A: By using a ruler!

Q: The nose is scared of going to school. Why?

A: He said that getting picked on is just too much.

Q: This kind of plate is used in Venus. What is it?

A: Flying saucers

Q: Teacher: Why are you all on the floor, doing your multiplication homework?

A: Student: Because you said that tables are not allowed.

Q: What did the number eight hear from the number zero?

A: Nice belt.

Q: At school, the favorite subject of a butterfly is?

A: Mothematics.

Q: The favorite sum of a math teacher is?

A: Summer!

Q: The 2 fours don't want dinner. Why?

A: Because they already ate.

Teacher: Answer at once, whatever I ask, okay? The total of eight and two is?

Class: At once!

Q: Math teachers prefer this type of meals. What is it?

A: Square meals!

Q: The quarter didn't accompany the nickel in rolling down the hill. Why?

A: Having more cents is his reason

Teacher: I hope I don't see you looking over at David's test.
Student: I hope you don't see me either.

Q: There once was a school just for elves and dwarves. What did they do after school every day?
A: They did their gnome work together.

Q: The lesson was written by the teacher on the glass window. Why?
A: So that the lesson will be very clear.

Teacher: If $20 is given each by five people, what will you get?
Student: Oh, I will surely get myself nice shoes.

Teacher: If I had six apples in my left hand and seven oranges in my right, what would I have?
Student: You would have two big hands.

Q: It was a very sunny and hot day. Why did the teacher go to the beach?
A: Because she wanted to test the water.

Teacher: Didn't you miss school yesterday?

Student: No, not really.

Q: The teacher always had her eyes crossed. Why?

A: Because her pupils cannot be controlled!

Q: Why are the sunglasses needed by the teacher?

A: The pupils in his class are so bright!

Computer Technology Jokes

Q: What kind of food do computers snack on?

A: Micro chips.

Q: How do computers make sweaters?

A: On the interknit.

Q: Why was the computer so thin?

A: Because it didn't have enough bytes.

Government Official: Why hasn't this rocket been sent into space yet?

Science Technician: The crew is on its launch break.

Roger: Did you hear that they are planning to put 500 cattle into orbit in space?

Randy: Yes, it will be the herd shot around the world.

Computer Clerk: What do you use in turning on your computer?

Customer: My right hand

Computer Clerk: That is amazing! People mostly use the off/on button!

Systems analyst: Your computer network needs an upgrade.

Business manager: Oh, this computer can't be rid of.

Systems analyst: Your operation will be way faster when the new system is installed. Why do you want to keep this old one?

Business manager: I think it knows too much.

Customer: A twig is found on the keyboard of the computer I bought yesterday.

Store Clerk: Our apologies, sir. It's best that you talk to our branch manager.

Student: I spent the entire night on my computer.

Mother: It will be more comfortable if you're in bed.

Q: The mattress that is overstuffed is so ecstatic. Why?

A: It's spring training time!

Critic: Did you say that your new play is about launching rockets into space?

Author: Yes. It uses three stages.

Q: If you happen to see a car with a kangaroo, what do you get?

A: A self-jump-starting car.

Mr. Lightbulb: Why do you need to see a doctor?

Mrs. Lightbulb: I'm experiencing hot flashes lately.

Q: A timepiece is with a fake friend. If you happen to see them, what do you get?
A: A two-faced clock.

Q: What do you get if you cross a camera with a firefly?
A: A shutterbug with a built-in flash.

Q: During dinner, what did the little train heard from his mother train?
A: Chew, chew!

Little watch: Please help me wash my face, mom.
Mama watch: I only have two hands, wait just a sec.

Computer teacher: Why are you bringing cheese into the computer room?
Student: You told me I was going to work with a mouse today!

Q: The telephone didn't want to go back to his home. Why?
A: Because joining a three-ring circus is his dream.

Everyday Silly Jokes and Riddles

Q: Why did the gentleman go crazy in the clothing store?

A: He was told it was a good place for a fit.

Q: What country is the best place to shop for neckwear?

A: Thailand.

Q: Music is made in the head by what?

A: A head band!

Q: What did the pen hear from the paper?

A: Certainly, write on!

Q: Before stealing gold and money, the robber first took a bath.
Why?

A: He needed a clean getaway.

Q: A snake's most musical part is?

A: The scales.

Q: Why is the man running around his bed?

A: He's trying to catch some sleep.

Q: How do you make a lemon drop?

A: You just drop it.

Q: The geologist heard this from the limestone. What is it?

A: Please don't take me for granite.

Q: What is bigger when it is upside down?

A: A 6.

Q: Billy went out with the prune. Why?

A: There is no date that he can find.

Q: The planets sing this kind of tune. What is it?

A: The planets sing Neptunes.

Q: The moon becomes the heaviest when?

A: During full moon.

Q: When looking for a job, this is where the seaweed goes. What is this place?

A: The kelp wanted section.

Q: How is the small flower called by the big flower?

A: Bud.

Q: What did Saturn hear from Mars?

A: Can I have a ring sometime?

Q: An ocean has this type of hair. What is it?

A: Wavy hair.

Q: You will know that the ocean is friendly by how?

A: By the way it waves.

Q: An attractive volcano is called what?

A: Lava-ble.

Q: What washes up on very small beaches?

A: Small beaches wash up microwaves.

Q: Why do you have to go to bed every evening?

A: The bed will not come to you.

Q: The music can't be listened to by the athlete. Why?

A: The record is broken because of her.

Q: Would you like to join me in a cup of tea?

A: Sure, but do you think we will both fit?

Q: When is a car door not really a car door?

A: When it's a jar.

Q: Do you know the best thing that Switzerland has?

A: There is a big plus on their flag.

Q: What did two walls say to each other?

A: See you at the corner.

Q: What is the reason behind the picture going to jail?

A: It's framed.

Q: What do toilets say to one another?

A: You look somewhat flushed.

Q: Where do an alien that weighs 500 pounds go?

A: It goes on a diet.

Q: Balloons are frightened with this type of music. What is it?

A: Balloons get scared of pop music.

Q: Why was the broom late?

A: The broom was late because it over swept.

Q: When Cinderella's pictures didn't show up, what did she say?

A: My prints will definitely come someday.

Q: During the day is the only time dragons sleep. Why?

A: They need to fight the knights.

Q: Why do bicycles always seem to fall over?

A: They are two tired.

Q: It dries up more the wetter it gets.

A: A towel.

Q: No one wants to talk to Lee, so what do you call him?

A: Lonely

Q: Were you long in the hospital?

A: No, I still have the same size.

Q: What goes ding dong and color blue?

A: An Avon lady at the North Pole

Q: What did the envelope hear from the stamp?

A: When we stick together, we can reach so many places.

Q: The laziest part of the car is called?

A: Wheels

Q: What has yellow wheels and is color green?

A: Grass. Sorry about lying about the wheels.

Q: Mickey Mouse took a trip to space. Why?

A: He is looking for Pluto.

Q: The calendar is so popular. Why?

A: It has so many dates.

Q: Your nose cannot be as long as 12 inches. Why?

A: It will become a foot.

Q: Writing with which hand is better?

A: Neither, writing with a pen is the best.

Q: What makes the newspaper different from the television?

A: Try swatting a fly using a television.

Q: April 1 makes everybody so tired. Why?

A: Finishing 31 days of March is so tiring.

Q: What is the reason that they arrested the belt?

A: Some pants were being held up by them.

Q: What did two elevators talk to each other?

A: I think I'm coming down with something!

Q: What did the impatient customer hear from the laundryman?

A: Keep your shirt on!

Q: Last night, there has been a robbery. Have you heard about it?

A: A pair of pants was held up by 2 clothespins.

Q: How can you cure a headache?

A: The pane will be gone if you put your head through a window.

Q: This object has flies and four wheels.

A: A garbage truck!

Q: The type of car that is driven by the wife of Mickey Mouse is called?

A: A minnie van!

Q: Traffic lights can't go swimming. Why?

A: Changing takes longer.

Q: It doesn't move but can go down and up. What is it?

A: Stairs

Q: Cards cannot be played by the pirates. Why?

A: Because the deck is where he was sitting.

Q: What is the reason Mozart let go of the chickens?

A: The chickens keep saying Bach, Bach, Bach!

Q: This thing is always overlooked, even by the most careful man.
What is it?

A: Their nose.

Q: The cold front's opposite is called?

A: A warm back.

Q: No one believes him but everyone is listening to him. Who is he?

A: The weather reporter.

Q: How hot is it?

A: If I got steam when I turn on my lawn sprinkler, then it is so hot.

Q: When a fog disperses in California, what happens?

A: U C LA

Q: What did the lightning bolt hear from the cloud?

A: Oh, you are shocking!

Q: Hurricanes can see because of this. What is it?

A: They use their single eye.

Q: This never hits the ground whenever it falls. What is it?

A: The temperature!

Q: This bow cannot be tied. What is it?

A: A rainbow!

Q: What did two volcanoes whisper to one another?

A: I lava you!

Q: The favorite game of a tornado is called?

A: Twister!

Q: Clouds wear this kind of shorts. What is it?

A: Thunderwear shorts.

Q: What did the sports car hear from the tornado?

A: Hey, let's go for a spin!

My wife is as cold as marble. She says I take her for granite!

Mr. and Mrs. Brown had 2 children. Both of them are boys. Their names are Trouble and Mind Your Own Business. Both of them decided to play the game hide-and-seek one beautiful day. Mind Your Own Business counted from one to one hundred while Trouble was looking for a place to hide. Mind Your Own Business went searching for his brother, Trouble, in every corner, even behind bushes and trash cans. He even looked in and under the cars so that he could find him. Suddenly, a policeman went to him. He asked him what he was doing. Mind Your Own Business replied, "I'm playing a game." "What game?" The officer asked. He replied, "Hide-and-Seek." The policeman then asked for his name. He answered, "Mind Your Own Business." That made the officer furious. "Are you looking for trouble?" the policeman asked. "Yes, I am," the boy replied.

Manicurist is my mother's occupation while my dad is a dentist. Tooth and nail they fought most of their married life.

Mom said we had to keep our grocery bills down. So I bought her a paperweight.

They finally invented a computer that is as smart as a person. It puts all the blame for its mistakes on another computer.

I was thinking the entire night on what place the sun goes to when it sets. It finally dawned on me.

I always have lunch at this Japanese fast food place. You only have to take off one shoe.

There is another family that goes to the same church my family goes as well. So, one day, my nephew decided that he will make some food for them. The food was prayed over by my nephew. He then asked his son, Miguel, aged 3 years old to bless the food as well. The boy then bowed his head and prayed, "Lord God, thank you that there is still some food left for us at our home. It wasn't given to them all."

One year, during Easter, I decided to visit my granddaughter named Julie. She was 5 years old. It's a holiday so I opted to put on my best suit. I was surprised by what she said when we met. Julie said, "You look so dashing today, Granpa. You took a shower, didn't you?"

I was working in construction during the late 1950s. The corner of the house that we are leveling up was just jacked above the ground for about 4 inches. The house suddenly went down causing a loud band when one of the jacks slipped. The minister, the owner of the house, suddenly ran out. He then looked at the heavens and exclaimed, "I thought Jesus was coming." We couldn't stop laughing after that.

One afternoon, a young girl climbed and sat on the lap of her grandfather. She then asked him if she were made by God. Her grandpa replied, "Yes." She asked again, "Are you made by God, too?" The grandfather answered yes again. Then, the girl went silent while looking at the thinning hair and wrinkles of his grandfather. Suddenly, she said, "Well, I guess nowadays, he's doing a much better job."

One sweltering day, some flower seeds were being planted by a young man in his garden. It was a very sunny day because of the hot sun, making the man all sweaty. His neighbor noticed him planting and said, "I recommend that those seeds should be planted when the sun has gone down or during the morning when it is still cool." The young man smiled and replied, "Thank you. However, the package says otherwise. It said to 'Plant in full sun', so I can't do what you recommended.

There is an easier method that you can use to differentiate a vegetable and a weed when your garden needs some weeding. It is a weed if it doesn't come up after you pull on it. It is not if it easily comes out.

I have a grandson that really loves trains. His name is Michael, and he is 6 years old. One day, I challenged him to name an old steam engine's different parts. He then told me that one part is called cowcatcher. I then asked him the uses of the cowcatcher. He replied, "It is used in catching cows and scooting them of the railways so that my grandfather wouldn't have the trouble of chasing them away.

My family and I were sitting at the dining table for dinner. My sister and my wife were brainstorming on recipes. A dump cake was one of the suggestions. Honey, my daughter who is 4 years old, suddenly exclaimed, "Eww! It already has garbage in it!"

I have a son named David. He was 5 years old and still going to the daycare. One day, he came to me and announced that he didn't want to go to his school anymore. I asked him, "Why?" He said his classmates are still kids. He told me that he is already a big boy, and he can stay alone at home while I go to work. I asked him then if you will be the one to make his lunch since he can't still reach the stove. He immediately answered, "I can eat salad."

Favorite Dad Jokes

Q: How will you use 2 matchsticks to start a fire?

A: Ensure that at least one is a match.

Q: How would you go about talking with a bunch of giants?

A: You use big words!

Q: If it is not your cheese, what do you call it?

A: Nacho cheese.

Q: What do you call your dad when he falls through the ice?

A: A Pop-sicle!

Q: Getting out of it is hard but getting into is easy.

A: Trouble.

Q: In a pint, how many peas are included?

A: Only one

Q: When you say it, it breaks. What is it?

A: Silence!

Q: When is the only time that work is behind success?

A: In the dictionary!

Q: It stays in place even if it always runs. It has a round face and two hands. What is it?

A: A clock!

Q: It can still hold water no matter how many holes it has.

A: A sponge!

Q: When is the only time that the horse is behind a cart?

A: In the dictionary!

Q: It contains a million letters, ends with a letter E, and begins with a letter P. What is it?

A: Post Office!

Q: Are holes present in your shirts?

A: No.

Then how did you put it on?

Q: Does a ton of bricks weigh more than a ton of feathers?

A: No. They have the same weight.

Q: Count the number of books you can put in a backpack that is empty.

A: One!

Q: Use two letters to spell rotted.

A: DK (decay)

Q: Count the months that have 28 days.

A: All of them!

Q: If you take more away from it, it only gets bigger and bigger. What is it?

A: A hole!

Q: This never comes down, but only goes up?

A: A person's age

Small monster says to his dad: "Dad, the dentist wasn't painless like he said he would be."

Dad monster: "Did he hurt you?"

Small monster: "No, but he yelled at me when I bit his finger."

Knock-knock – "Who's there?" -- Butcher – Butcher who?

A: Butcher right foot in, butcher right foot out, butcher right foot in and shake it all about; butcher left foot in, butcher left foot out, butcher left foot in and shake it all about!

Dad: "Hello, my name is Cliff. Why don't you drop over and come see me sometime?"

Kid: "Dad did you get a haircut?"
Dad: "No, I got them all cut."

Q: What is the reason behind the cookie crying?
A: It has been so long since his father was a wafer.

Q: How many apples grow on a tree?
A: All of them.

Dad: My son got an "A" for cutting class.
Neighbor: How could that happen? What school does he go to?
Dad: Barber school.

Q: Have you heard the roof joke?
A: Forget it. It's over your head!

Q: Count the letters in the Alphabet.
A: It contains 11 letters.

Q: Use two letters to spell cold.

A: IC

Q: Most water surrounds this state. What is it?

A: Hawaii

Q: The father of David has three boys named Crackle, Snap, and?

A: David!

Q: What will your place be in the race if you passed the man in the second place?

A: 2nd place!

Q: Name the gravity's center.

A: It's the letter V.

Q: This word in English has 3 consecutive double letters. What is it?

A: Bookkeeper

Q: This object is brown, has no legs, has a tail, and a head. What is it?

A: A penny.

Did you hear about the day the computer at the office broke down and everybody had to think?

My son wrote home from college the other day that he has grown another foot. His grandmother knit him the third sock!

The gosling never believed a word his father said. As far as he was concerned, it was all papaganda.

When the grocery store clerk asks my dad if he wants the milk in a bag, he always replies: "No, I'd like the milk in the container, please."

People are always calling me a hypochondriac. Let me tell you, it makes me sick!

Did you hear about the comedian who told the same joke three nights running? I guess he wouldn't dare tell it standing still!

I am so unlucky that I get paper cuts from get-well cards.

My sister is so lazy. She puts popcorn in the flapjack batter so the pancakes flip themselves!

A horseback riding school was recently opened by a guy. I heard the business fell off.

There are a lot of things money cannot buy. None of them are on my son's wish list.

Q: What do you call a superhero who loves ice cream?

A: A scooper-hero!

Food Jokes

Q: You can make this yummy cheese backward. What is it?

A: Edam.

Q: What is something you can never have for lunch or dinner?

A: Breakfast

Q: Name the favorite drink of a boxer.

A: Any kind of punch.

Q: What famous author wrote plays about fruit?

A: William Shakes-pear.

Q: What kind of breakfast cereal do you get when your pet bird flies into a fan?

A: Shredded tweet!

Q: Why was the oil and vinegar late for dinner?

A: Because they were dressing.

Q: What happened with the student chef who made a mess of an omelet in cooking school?

A: She was egg-spelled.

Q: What made the cookie cry?

A: Because its mother had been a wafer so long.

Q: Why did the doughnut baker close up his shop?

A: Because he was fed up with the hole business.

Q: A fake noodle's other name.

A: An impasta.

Q: There has been a race between the tomato and the lettuce. Have you heard about it?

A: The tomato was trying to catch up while the lettuce was a head.

Q: What famous author wrote poetry about French fries?

A: Edgar Allan Poe-tato.

Q: Where do smart hotdogs end up?

A: On an honor roll.

Q: Why did the potato have a black eye?

A: It got in the way of the fruit punch.

Q: This is used by the little fruit to shave itself.

A: A raisin blade.

Q: What is the worst kind of cake to have?

A: A stomachache.

Q: When the orange fell from the tree, why did it roll a little and then suddenly stop?

A: It ran out of juice.

Q: Where is the best place to find out the exact weight of the pie?

A: Way up high.

Q: What did the bored cola bottles do for excitement?

A: They played Follow the Liter.

Q: What does a seven-foot tall butcher weigh?

A: Meat.

Q: How do vegetables travel from field to field?

A: They take a taxi cabbage.

Seasonal Jokes

Q: What happened to the witch when her broomstick broke and she could no longer get around?

A: She witch-hiked.

Q: On Valentine's Day, this is what the valentine of the light bulb heard from him. What is it?

A: I love you watts and watts.

Q: What kind of plant do you get when you plant kisses?

A: You get the plant two lips.

Q: What does the Easter bunny do to stay in shape?

A: The Easter Bunny does lots of eggcercise to stay in shape.

Q: A four-leaf clover shouldn't be ironed. Why?

A: Your luck might be pressed.

Q: Where does the Easter Bunny go for breakfast?

A: The Easter Bunny goes for breakfast at IHOP.

Q: Name the favorite fruit of a scarecrow.

A: A scarecrow's favorite fruit is strawberries, of course.

Q: When will you be unlucky meeting a black cat?

A: If you're a mouse

Q: What is behind the noises in graveyards?

A: It is because of all the coffins.

Q: The road can't be crossed by the zombie? Why?

A: He has no guts.

Q: When a vampire has no mate, what is it called?

A: A bat-chelor.

Q: Why did the baby ghost seem so sad?

A: The baby ghost just wanted his mummy.

Q: What do witches put on their bagels?

A: Oh, witches put scream cheese on their bagels.

Q: What do you call a pretty witch who is also nice and friendly?

A: That's what you call failure.

Q: What did the vampire think about Dracula the movie?

A: He thought the movie was fangtastic.

Q: Why is it that vampires are hard to get along with?

A: Because they are a pain in the neck!

Q: What will you do to make the witch itch?

A: You just need to remove the w.

Q: What class is the witch's favorite subject in school?

A: Spelling.

Q: Who will be the Thanksgiving band's drummer?

A: The turkey has the drumsticks.

Q: Who doesn't feel like eating on Thanksgiving?

A: The stuffed turkey.

Q: How do you send a turkey through the mail in time for Thanksgiving?

A: You send the turkey through bird class.

Q: After getting into a fight, what happened to the turkey?

A: The stuffing got knocked out of the turkey.

Q: What is the worst kind of key to use for opening doors?

A: A Tur-key.

Q: What does the Invisible Man think of his mother and father?

A: He thinks they are a pair of transparents.

Q: What is the favorite day of the cow out of the whole year?

A: A cow is a big fan of Moo Year's Day!

Q: Why does everyone always do so poorly after Thanksgiving?

A: Because everything in the world gets marked down after the holidays.

Q: What is the Christmas song that Tarzan loved to sing?

A: Tarzan always sings Jungle Bells around Christmas.

Q: This is the preferred breakfast meal of snowmen. What is it?

A: Frosted Snow Flakes.

Q: What is the favorite Christmas song of a parent?

A: Oh, Silent Night.

Q: What is a fake stone that exists in Ireland called?

A: A sham rock.

Q: Why did Santa and his reindeer get a ticket on Christmas Eve?

A: Because their sleigh is left on a snow-parking zone.

Q: Do female deer admire Mrs. Claus?

A: Oh yes, they fawn all over her!

Q: Why is Rudolph so good at playing trivia?

A: Rudolph is good at playing trivia because he nose a lot and is very bright!

Q: Where does Santa store his suit after Christmas?

A: In the claus-it!

Q: What is an ig?

A: It is an igloo without the toilet!

Knock-Knock Jokes

"Knock, Knock"

"Who's there?"

Abba.

Abba who?

Abba banana!

"Knock, Knock"

"Who's there?"

Abbey.

Abbey who?

Abbey stung me on my nose!

"Knock, Knock"

"Who's there?"

Abbott.

Abbott who?

Abbott time you answered my call!

"Knock, Knock"

"Who's there?"

Bacon.

Bacon who?

Bacon a pretty cake for the celebration.

"Knock, Knock"

"Who's there?"

Adam.

Adam who?

Adam up. The sum is the answer.

"Knock, Knock"

"Who's there?"

Canoe.

Canoe who?

Canoe you play this game with me?

"Knock, Knock"

"Who's there?"

Carmen.

Carmen who?

Carmen get it.

"Knock, Knock"

"Who's there?"

Carl.

Carl who?

Carl not run if you keep pressing the brakes.

"Knock, Knock"
"Who's there?"
A.C.
A.C. who?
A.C. come, A.C. go

Know, Knock
"Who's there?"
Luke
Luke who?
Luke over here and see what I'm talking about

"Knock, Knock"
"Who's there?"
Armageddon.
Armageddon who?
Armageddon happy with all these gifts?

"Knock, Knock"
"Who's there?"
Recycle
Recycle who?
Recycle around the city in our car.

"Knock, Knock"

"Who's there?"

Hank.

Hank who?

You're welcome

"Knock, Knock"

"Who's there?"

Quacker.

Quacker who?

Quacker nother joke and I'm leaving!

"Knock, Knock"

"Who's there?"

Xavier.

Xavier who?

Xavier your toys and give them to the homeless.

Occupation Jokes

Q: How is your job at the travel agency?

A: Terrible. I am not going anywhere.

Q: What do you call a person who makes miniature watches?

A: A small-time operator.

Q: Why does the custodian always wait until 11:00 a.m. to clean the floors on the weekend?

A: Because he likes to sweep late on Saturday mornings.

Q: Glasses are worn by the teacher. Why?

A: She has so many bright students.

Q: What happened to the couch potato who used to sell furniture in this store?

A: He got sacked.

Q: What kind of business did Mr. Gopher startup?

A: A hole-sale business.

Q: What is the biggest problem miners have?

A: Coal feet.

Q: An underwater spy is called?

A: James Pond!

Q: When is the time that a doctor gets mad?

A: When he runs out of patients.

Q: Who has the easiest job in the world?

A: Candle makers have the easiest job in the world. They work only on wick ends.

Q: Why was there lightning and thunder in the laboratory?

A: The scientists were brainstorming.

Q: Have you heard that gossip about the germ?

A: Forget it. I don't want that to spread out.

Q: There's a ringing sound I keep hearing, Doctor.

A: You should answer your phone.

Q: I think I'm a moth, Doctor.

A: Please get out of my light.

Q: Patient: I sometimes feel like I'm invisible, Doctor.

A: Doctor: Who said that?

Q: What did two tonsils say on each other?

A: Get dressed up, the doctor is taking us out!

Q: When a boat is sick, where does it go?

A: To the dock!

Q: Why did the doctor lose his temper?

A: Because he has no patients anymore.

Q: The pillow went to the doctor's office. Why?

A: He was feeling all stuffed up!

Q: Why did the cookie feel like it had to go to the hospital?

A: Sadly, the cookie was feeling a little crummy.

Q: How do put the baby of an astronaut to sleep?

A: You rocket.

Q: An actor fell through the floorboards.

A: He was just going through a stage.

Q: What award did the dentist get?

A: A little plaque

Q: Does your tooth still hurt?

A: I'm not sure, the dentist kept it.

Q: What is the favorite animal of a dentist?

A: A molar bear.

Q: What did the dentist hear from the tooth when it was leaving?

A: When you get back, fill me in.

Q: When there is an earthquake, what does the dentist do?

A: She braces herself!

Q: This is the best time to visit a dentist.

A: Tooth-Hurty.

Q: The king went to the dentist. Why?

A: He wants his teeth crowned.

Q: The tree went to the dentist. Why?

A: He wants his root canal removed.

Q: What did the dentist hear from the judge?

A: Do you swear to pull the tooth, the whole tooth, and nothing but
the tooth?

Q: What did two teeth say to each other?

A: Thar's gold in them fills.

Q: Why did the nurse carry around a red pen?

A: So she could draw blood.

Q: Did you hear that the farmer down the road is not going to grow carrots any longer?

A: He said the carrots are long enough.

Q: A nurse walked into the busy office of the doctor and said, "Doctor, the Invisible Man is here."

A: "Sorry, I can't see him," replied the doctor.

Customer: My watch only runs every other day.

Salesperson: It was probably made by a part-time employee.

Q: What is the favorite song of all electrical engineers?

A: Ohm on the Range

Reporter: What is it like to be an astronaut?

Astronaut: It is a little weird. It is really the only job in the world where you get fired before you go to work.

Q: If an athlete's foot is for athletes, then what is for astronauts?

A: Missile toe.

Mr. Crow: I do not really feel like going to work today!
Mrs. Crow: Well, caw in sick.

Q: The favorite day of the week of a monk is?
A: Friarday.

Q: Why was the catamaran boat so upset?
A: He was docked a day's pay.

Sam: Hello Jerry! I haven't seen you in ages. How is your business?
Tom: Oh, it couldn't be better, Sam. I am always looking at piles of money!
Sam: Really, how do you do it?
Tom: I'm a bank teller.

Harry: You should really hire Joe to represent you in your lawsuit.
Mary: Joe? Why him? He graduated at the bottom of his law school class. I don't think he has ever won a case.
Harry: True, but he will lose for you cheaper than anyone else in town.

Boss: You never do some work and yet you want a raise? You've got the nerve!

Employee: Let's just say that the others have no extra burden when I went on a vacation.

Q: How is the job going?
A: I had to quit due to illness and fatigue.
Q: Oh. The boss was sick and tired of you, huh?

Mr. Green: Why is the chimney sweep so happy?
Mr. White: It's flue season!

Reporter: Can you tell me about your tennis ball company not doing well?
Business person: Yes. It will bounce back.

Some Silly Titles of Books

Don't Leave Without Me by Isa Coming

Tape Recording for Beginners by Cass Ette

The Terrible Problem by Major Setback

My Golden Wedding by Annie Versary

A Call for Assistance by Linda Hand

Water Garden Features by Lily Pond

Will He Win? By Betty Wont

Making the Least of Life by Minnie Mumm

Making the Most of Life by Maxie Mumm

Truthful Tales by Frank Lee

The Haunted Room by Hugo First

The Winning Game by Vic Tree

Beginning Magic by Beatrix Star

Dangerous Germs by Mike Robes

Grand Canyon Adventures by Rhoda Donkey

The Garlic Eater by I. Malone

How to Make Money by Robin Banks

Hide and Seek by I.C. Hugh

Season's Greetings by Mary Christmas

The Wrong Shoe by Titus Canbe

The Ghost of a Witch by Eve L. Spirit

Reaching the Top by Ella Vator

Boo! By Terry Fied

My Crystal Ball by C.A. Lot

Making Enemies to Lose Friends by Olive Alone

Heat Your House in Winter by Ray D. Ater

Silly Slogans and Signs

Repeated with pride by all of the most observant Dads!

Picture Frame Store: We want to hang around your house.

Rope Company: If you can't afford a clothes dryer, inquire about a credit line.

Thermostat Company: Install one of our thermostats, and you'll never have to worry about your home cooking.

Famous Glue Company: Customers always stick with us.

Furnas Company: We are proud to be full of hot air.

Shoelace Company: We are truly fit to be tied.

Rope Inc.: Knot your ordinary company.

On a honey farm: You will like our grade of honey. It's bee plus!

In a bankrupt bakery: No dough!

On a rodeo gate: Bronc riders needed immediately, big bucks possible!

In the window of a pillow and comforter store: For sale – all it takes is a small down payment.

In the window of a health food restaurant: All you should eat: $3.50

In the gym's window: The weak ends here!

On the door of a police detective: Out to hunch.

In a cheese plant: We never lie about our aging.

In a bowling alley: Win some pin money when you sign up for our cash prize tournament.

Tire Company: Our tires will give your car good traction on wet roads. We skid you not!

On a travel agency: When we say that we want you to go away, we mean it!

In a fish factory: Many are cod, but few are frozen.

Sports Jokes

Q: Why does the baseball stadium always feel cold?

A: Because it is full of fans.

Q: When a baseball pitcher throws, why does he raise one leg?

A: When both of his legs are raised, he would fall.

Q: What job did Dracula get with the Transylvanian baseball team?

A: Bat boy.

Q: Why is bowling a quiet sport?

A: A pin drop can be heard.

Q: Where do football players dance?

A: At a foot ball.

Q: The fans of the Brazilian soccer are called what?

A: Brazil nuts!

Q: Why does a polo player ride a horse?

A: Because they are too heavy to carry.

Q: The favorite teams of hens are encouraged by how?

A: They keep on egging on them.

Q: Who won the race between two balls of string?

A: They were tied.

Q: Baseball games aren't liked by grasshoppers. Why?

A: Cricket is their preferred game.

Q: When we play a game with big cats, why do we need to be careful?

A: They might be cheetahs.

Q: What is the favorite color of a cheerleader?

A: Yeller.

Q: Name the skydiving's hardest part?

A: The ground!

Q: Why did the man keep doing the backstroke?

A: Because his stomach is so full after eating so much.

Q: Magicians and hockey players have this similarity. What is it?

A: The two of them do hat tricks!

Q: What is the favorite sport of an insect?

A: Cricket!

Q: Why did the ballerina quit?

A: Because it was tu-tu hard!

Q: Tarzan loves spending time on a golf course. Why?

A: He wants to perfect his swing.

Q: Tennis is a really loud sport. Why?

A: A racquet is raised by the players.

Q: The faster you ran, the harder it is to catch. What is it?

A: Your breath

Q: Why did the football coach go to the bank?

A: The coach wants to have his quarter back.

Q: To stay cool, baseball players do this. What is it?

A: They sit next to the fans.

Q: Waiters is very good in what kind of sport?

A: Tennis, since they are good at serving.

Q: When it comes to hitting a baseball, what animal is the best?

A: A bat!

Q: The favorite letter of a golfer is?

A: Tee!

Q: What is the similarity between a pancake and a baseball team?

A: A good batter is what they both need.

Q: Why are two pairs of pants worn by the golfer?

A: In case he got a hole in one!

Q: A basketball-playing pig is called?

A: A ball hog.

Q: Donuts are loved by basketball players. Why?

A: Because they can dunk them.

Q: What is the reason why the basketball player is sent to jail?

A: The ball is shot because of him.

Q: What time is the baby good at basketball?

A: When the baby is dribbling.

Q: Soccer can't be played by Cinderella. Why?

A: She always runs away from the ball.

Q: What is the favorite food of a cheerleader?

A: Cheerios.

Q: What are four bullfighters that are in a quicksand called?

A: Quattro sinko.

Q: A not working boomerang is called?

A: A stick.

Q: The favorite position of a ghost in soccer is called?

A: Ghoul keeper.

Conclusion

Thank you so much for making it through to the end of this book. I hope it was informative and able to provide you with all of the tools you need to learn about, tell, and share funny dad jokes. The next step is to start trying out some of the jokes described here in your own life. Practice reading them out loud. Try to memorize them. If you are able to, talk to your own dad and see what jokes are funniest to him. If you are a dad yourself, you might try some of these out on your friends, family, co-workers, or your own kids. If you have a dad, try your hand at making him laugh at the banal and absurd. See if you can make him laugh as much as he can make you and others laugh, hand to forehead groan, and eye roll with a head shake. Experience familiar and famous puns repeated in their own unique manner here within the intimacy of your own family. These jokes should make you laugh, celebrate, and agree that dads and silly, pun-tastic jokes go hand-in-hand. We don't always know what makes Dad tick, but we do know he has the time of his life starting the day with a good joke, pranking his best friend, or embarrassing his kids over and over again. Have fun with the jokes in this book. Say them aloud to your best friend, teacher, or dad himself. Celebrate Dad with his innate ability and desire to make light of anything and everything. It is just what dads do. We love them all the more for it. If you enjoyed this book, please take the time to rate it on Amazon. Your honest review would be greatly appreciated. Thank you!

Connect with us on our Facebook page www.facebook.com/bluesourceandfriends and stay tuned to our latest book promotions and free giveaways.

Karen J. Bun

9 781797 925561